Non-Continental

Alaska
Hawaii

David Petechuk

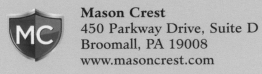

Mason Crest
450 Parkway Drive, Suite D
Broomall, PA 19008
www.masoncrest.com

©2016 by Mason Crest, an imprint of National Highlights, Inc.

Printed and bound in the United States of America.

CPSIA Compliance Information: Batch #LES2015.
For further information, contact Mason Crest at 1-866-MCP-Book.

First printing
1 3 5 7 9 8 6 4 2

Library of Congress Cataloging-in-Publication Data

Petechuk, David.
 Non-continental : Alaska, Hawaii / David Petechuk.
   pages cm. — (Let's explore the states)
 Includes bibliographical references and index.
 ISBN 978-1-4222-3328-3 (hc)
 ISBN 978-1-4222-8613-5 (pb)
 1. Alaska—Juvenile literature. 2. Hawaii—Juvenile literature. I. Title.
 F904.3.P39 2016
 979.8—dc23
                          2015008412

Let's Explore the States series ISBN: 978-1-4222-3319-1

About the Author: David Petechuk is a freelance writer and independent scholar. A former director of publications at a major medical center, he has written books on the respiratory system and transplantation ethics, as well as a book about LSD for a drug information series targeting middle school students.

Picture Credits: Office of the Governor of Hawaii: 55; Hawaiian State Archives: 48; Library of Congress: 10, 19, 20, 21, 22, 28 (top), 56 (top); National Archives: 49 (top); National Maritime Museum, Greenwich, UK: 46; used under license from Shutterstock, Inc.: 1, 5, 6, 7, 9, 14, 15, 16, 17, 25, 27, 30, 31, 34, 35, 37, 38 (bottom), 40, 41, 42, 45, 54 (bottom), 57, 58, 60; Eric Broder Van Dyke / Shutterstock.com: 53; Steve Broer / Shutterstock.com: 26; EpicStockMedia / Shutterstock.com: 38 (top); Featureflash / Shutterstock.com: 28 (bottom); Jose Gil / Shutterstock.com: 54 (top); Jeffrey T. Kreulen / Shutterstock.com: 12 (bottom); Nimon / Shutterstock.com: 49 (bottom); Ruth Peterkin / Shutterstock.com: 12 (top); Theodore Trimmer / Shutterstock.com: 50; Jeff Whyte / Shutterstock.com: 47, 51; U.S. Fish and Wildlife Service: 13; U.S. Senate collection: 52; White House photo: 56 (bottom).

Table of Contents

KEY ICONS TO LOOK FOR:

Words to Understand: These words with their easy-to-understand definitions will increase the reader's understanding of the text, while building vocabulary skills.

Sidebars: This boxed material within the main text allows readers to build knowledge, gain insights, explore possibilities, and broaden their perspectives by weaving together additional information to provide realistic and holistic perspectives.

Research Projects: Readers are pointed toward areas of further inquiry connected to each chapter. Suggestions are provided for projects that encourage deeper research and analysis.

Text-Dependent Questions: These questions send the reader back to the text for more careful attention to the evidence presented there.

Series Glossary of Key Terms: This back-of-the book glossary contains terminology used throughout this series. Words found here increase the reader's ability to read and comprehend higher-level books and articles in this field.

LET'S EXPLORE THE STATES

Atlantic: North Carolina, Virginia, West Virginia

Central Mississippi River Basin: Arkansas, Iowa, Missouri

East South-Central States: Kentucky, Tennessee

Eastern Great Lakes: Indiana, Michigan, Ohio

Gulf States: Alabama, Louisiana, Mississippi

Lower Atlantic: Florida, Georgia, South Carolina

Lower Plains: Kansas, Nebraska

Mid-Atlantic: Delaware, District of Columbia, Maryland

Non-Continental: Alaska, Hawaii

Northern New England: Maine, New Hampshire, Vermont

Northeast: New Jersey, New York, Pennsylvania

Northwest: Idaho, Oregon, Washington

Rocky Mountain: Colorado, Utah, Wyoming

Southern New England: Connecticut, Massachusetts, Rhode Island

Southwest: New Mexico, Oklahoma, Texas

U.S. Territories and Possessions

Upper Plains: Montana, North Dakota, South Dakota

The West: Arizona, California, Nevada

Western Great Lakes: Illinois, Minnesota, Wisconsin

 Alaska at a Glance

Area: 665,384 sq mi (1,723,336 sq km). Largest state.[1]
  Land: 570,641 sq mi (1,477,950 sq km)
  Water: 94,743 sq miles (245,383 sq km)
Highest elevation: Denali (Mount McKinley), 20,237 feet (6,168 m)
Lowest elevation: sea level (Pacific Ocean)

Statehood: Jan. 3, 1959 (49th state)
Capital: Juneau
Population: 736,732
    (48th largest state)[2]

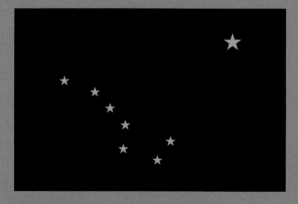

State nickname: The Last Frontier
State bird: Willow Ptarmigan
State flower: Forget-me-not

[1] *U.S. Census Bureau*
[2] *U.S. Census Bureau, 2014 estimate*

Alaska

T alk about big! Not only is Alaska the largest of all the U.S. states, Alaska also contains a lot of big things. Denali (also known as Mount McKinley) is the highest mountain peak in North America. Alaska is home to the largest national park in the United States, Wrangell-Saint Elias (13.2 million acres), and the country's largest national forest, Tongass (nearly 17 million acres). Alaska also has the world's longest chain of active volcanoes.

The state's abundance of wildlife includes major populations of bald eagles and salmon. Alaska is also home to more bears than any other state. It has an estimated 200,000 black bears, nearly five times the number of bears than the next closest state (Wisconsin). In addition, Alaska is home to approximately 30,000 grizzly bears.

Geography

Alaska covers approximately 665,384 square miles (1,723,336 square kilometers). It is more than twice the size of the second-largest state, Texas.

Water surrounds most of Alaska, which has approximately 6,640 miles of coastline. Alaska is bordered to the north by the Arctic Ocean, which includes the Beaufort Sea and the Chukchi Sea. The south is bordered by the Gulf of Alaska and the Pacific Ocean. The Bering Sea is to the west. The eastern and part of the southern part of Alaska is bordered by Canada's Yukon Territory and British Columbia.

Alaska's geography can be categorized into four main areas: two mountain ranges, a central plateau, and the

Words to Understand in This Chapter

Athabaskan—A speaker of a family of North American Indian languages.

Eskimo—member of an indigenous people inhabiting Alaska, as well as northern Canada, Greenland, and eastern Siberia; the term is commonly used in Alaska to refer to all Inuit and Yupik people.

Eyak—an indigenous group of people traditionally located on the Copper River Delta and near the town of Cordova, Alaska.

Inuit—group of culturally similar indigenous peoples found in the Arctic regions of North America and Greenland.

migration—movement of people or animals from one region or country to another.

negligence—failure to take proper care when performing an action; can result in a court case when resulting in damage or injury.

permafrost—a thick layer of soil below the surface that remains frozen year round; occurs primarily in polar regions.

plain—a large area of land that is flat or rolling and has no trees.

plaintiff—a person or group who brings a court case against another person or group.

spawn—in the animal world the release or deposit of eggs.

Tlingit—indigenous people of the Pacific Northwest Coast of North America.

tributary—a river, creek, or stream flowing into a larger lake or river.

Arctic slope or coastal *plain*. The south and southeastern portion of Alaska lie within the Pacific Mountain System. This system is a series of mountain ranges that run along the Pacific Coast of North America, from British Columbia down the western coast of the United States and into northwestern Mexico.

Moving northward, the central and largest part of Alaska is the Central Uplands and Lowlands, which lie between the Alaska Range of the

Did You Know?

The name "Alaska" is believed to be derived from the Aleut Indian word *alyeska*, which means "great land."

Pacific Mountain System to the south and the Brooks Range of the Rocky Mountain System to the north. This area features rolling hills and swampy river valleys, including the Koyukuk,

Humpback whales play in the ocean near Juneau.

Alpine lakes and forest in Denali National Park.

Kuskokwim, Tanana, and Yukon River valleys.

The Rocky Mountain System is north of the Central Uplands and Lowlands and includes the Brooks Range and the Brooks Range foothills. The Brooks Range was formed by glaciers and includes peaks that rise 9,000 feet (2,700 m) above sea level.

The Arctic Coastal Plain covers the northernmost portion of Alaska and is a treeless plain that slopes toward the Arctic Ocean. The area features a permanently frozen ground known as *permafrost*. In the spring, some areas defrost enough to allow grass and wildflowers to grow. This area is called the tundra.

The Yukon River runs from Atlin Lake in British Columbia through Canada's Yukon Territory and throughout central Alaska, traveling from east to west. At 1,980 miles (3,187 km), the Yukon, which is believed to come from the Indian word for "big river," is the longest river in North America.

The second longest river in Alaska is the Kuskokwim River, which runs

Did You Know?

In Barrow, the sun sets in November and does not rise again until the middle of January.

for 702 miles (1,130 km). The river's headwaters are in the Kuskokwim Mountains and the Alaska Range. It runs to Kuskokwim Bay on the Bering Sea bordering western Alaska. The river's name is believed to be a loose translation from the Yupik word for "big, slow-moving thing."

Other notable Alaskan rivers include the Colville River, which begins in the De Long Mountains above the article circle. Frozen for more than six months a year, the river is used as a highway in the winter.

The Copper River is 300 miles (483 km) long and is named for the copper deposits found along its banks in the upper regions of the river. The river features an extensive delta and is also known for the more than two million wild salmon that *spawn* upstream

Passengers aboard a cruise ship enjoy the scenery in Glacier Bay National Park and Preserve.

Point Retreat Lighthouse sits below a glacier in Juneau, Alaska.

each year from mid-May through September. The Copper River Delta spans 700,000 acres.

Alaska also has many lakes. The largest is Iliamna Lake, which is 80 miles (129 km) long and 25 miles (40 km) wide. Iliamna Lake is the second-largest lake that lies completely within the borders of the United States, behind only Lake Michigan.

Becharof Lake is 27 miles (44 km) long and 15 miles (24 km) wide and is the second-largest lake in Alaska. The lake serves as a nursery for the world's second-largest sockeye salmon run. Each year, the lake and its *tributaries* provide up to six million adult salmon to the Bristol Bay fishery.

Aleknagik Lake in southwestern Alaska is about 20 miles (32 km) long and 16 miles (26 km) wide. Its name is believed to come from the Yupik word meaning "wrong way home." Lake Clark is about 42 miles (68 km) long and eight miles (13 km) wide and is located in southern Alaska.

Lake Minchumina is about nine miles long and six miles wide. The lake's location at almost the exact center of Alaska made it an important midway point for sled trail mail transportation in the 1920s and 1930s. It

A polar bear walks along the Beaufort Sea coastline of Alaska. This area is part of the Arctic National Wildlife Refuge (ANWR), a pristine region in northeastern Alaska that covers 19.2 million acres. ANWR has been protected from development since 1960, although in recent years some have pushed for oil exploration in this vast region.

also served as a landing stop for airplane transportation between the cities of Fairbanks and McGrath.

Alaska has 39 different mountain ranges, which include 17 of the highest peaks in the United States. Perhaps the best-known range is the Alaska Range, which stretches across southern Alaska. This range includes Denali (also known as Mount McKinley), which is approximately 20,237 feet (6,168 m) above sea level, making it the highest point in North America. The Alaska Range also includes several other peaks that surpass 13,000 feet (3,962 m).

The Alaska Peninsula and the Aleutian Islands are linked by the Aleutian Range in southwest Alaska. Known for its many active volcanoes,

In 2013, the Alaskan government announced that the height of Denali, or Mount McKinley, was about 83 feet (26 m) lower than previously believed. The name Denali *comes from the Athabaska language, and means "the high one."*

Dall sheep live in the mountainous areas of Alaska.

the mainland range covers 600 miles (966 km). The Aleutian Islands are a partially submerged western extension of the range featuring 14 large islands and about 55 small islands that stretch for another 1,000 miles (1,600 km).

The Brooks Range in the far north of Alaska is the northernmost extension of the Rocky Mountains in northern Alaska. Covering about 600 miles (966 km), the Brooks Range is the highest mountain range within the Arctic Circle. The highest points in the range are between 8,500 to 9,000 feet (2,591 to 2,743 m) and are found near the Canadian border in the west.

The St. Elias Mountain Range is a segment of the Pacific Coast ranges and is found in southeastern Alaska, as well as in Canada in the southwestern Yukon and northwestern part of British Columbia. The range includes many peaks that exceed 17,000 feet (5,180 m). Mount St. Elias stands at 18,008 feet (5,488 m), making it the second-highest point in North America.

The Alaska Coast Range is part of the Pacific Coast Ranges of western North America and extends from the British Columbia Coast Range in the South to the Saint Elias Range and Icefield Range in the North. In Alaska, the range's topography goes from sea level to icecaps rising 3,500 feet. Many peaks are around 8,000 feet. Mount Fairweather at 15,000 feet is the highest peak in the Alaskan portion of range.

Alaska features long days in the

Aurora borealis (or northern lights) illuminate the sky near Fairbanks. This natural light phenomenon is often seen in the high latitudes of the Arctic Circle.

summer. During the weeks prior to late June's summer solstice, daylight lasts anywhere from 18 to 21 hours, depending on the part of the state. However, in the winter, Alaska has extremely short days. At the time of the winter solstice on December 21, the southern and central portions of Alaska have anywhere from just under four hours of daylight to approximately six-and-a-half hours of daylight. North of the Arctic Circle, Alaska has 67 days of complete darkness.

Although Alaska is often thought of as a frigid part of the country in the winter, some places, such as Anchorage, have a warmer climate than "lower 48" cities such as Chicago. However, the interior part of Alaska, which includes the city of Fairbanks, can experience temperatures of –30° Fahrenheit (–34° Celsius) for several weeks at a time.

Alaska has monthly average temperatures ranging from 72°F (22°C) in the summer to a low of –22°F (–30°C) in the winter, depending on the area. The highest temperature ever recorded in Alaska was 100°F (38°C),

An American bald eagle lands on a signpost in Homer. Alaska is home to more bald eagles than any other U.S. state.

recorded on June 27, 1915 at Fort Yukon. The lowest temperature was –80°F (–62 °C) recorded at Prospect Creek Camp in the Endicott Mountains of northern Alaska on January 23, 1971.

Alaska gets plenty of snowfall, but amounts vary according to region. Snowfall is least extreme in the southeastern portion of Alaska and on the North Slope (on the northern slope of the Brooks Range), where the extreme cold prevents high amounts of snowfall. Snowfall there averages about 25 to 30 inches (64 to 77 cm) a year.

Anchorage has an average annual snowfall of 79 inches (201 cm). However, the city of Talkeetna, which is just two hours to the north of Anchorage, is at a higher elevation and has an annual snowfall of about 138 inches (350 cm) annually.

The most snowfall occurs along the south coast of Alaska. For example, the seaside community of Valdez in southeastern Alaska is known as the snow capital of Alaska. Valdez has an average snowfall of more than 300 inches (760 cm) per year.

History

The oldest existing sites of proven human occupation in Alaska date back 11,000 years. Most archaeologists believe that humans arrived in this region even earlier. Overall, it is believed that three major *migrations* of people to Alaska took place.

The first humans probably entered Alaska from Asia via a land bridge that connected Alaska and Siberia. At the time, the sea level was much lower than it is today. This migration likely occurred at least 15,000 years ago, but some scientists believe it may have taken place more than 25,000 years ago. These humans spread throughout North and South America. They are believed to be the ancestors of most Native American tribes.

A second migration is took place somewhere between 9,000 and 14,000 years ago. These people came from the northeastern forests of Siberia. They are believed to be the ancestors of Native Alaskan tribes like the *Tlingit*, *Eyak*, and *Athabaskans*. A third migration likely occurred about 6,000 to 10,000 years ago. The immigrants came from the coast of northeast Siberia and are the ancestors of the *Eskimo* and Aleuts.

The first record of Europeans arriving in Alaska dates to 1741. The

Alaskan mainland and the Aleutian Islands were discovered by a Russian named Alexei Chirkov and a Dane named Vitus Bering, who was working for the Russian Empire. They encountered several of Alaska's Native American tribes, including the Aleuts, Eskimos, and Athabaskans. At the time, about 15,000 Aleuts lived in the Aleutian Island chain and the southernmost portion of Alaska. Eskimos lived throughout Alaska, primarily along the coasts. The Athabaskans lived in small groups of 15 to 75 people and inhabited Alaska's vast interior. Chirkov and Bering claimed the territory for the Russian Empire.

Alaska was still largely unexplored when U.S. Secretary of State William Seward arranged to buy the vast region from Russia for $7.2 million in 1867. Although the price amounted to only about two cents per acre, some members of the U.S. Congress ridiculed the purchase, which became known as "Seward's folly."

Alaska remained largely ignored after its purchase by the United

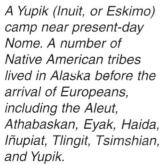

A Yupik (Inuit, or Eskimo) camp near present-day Nome. A number of Native American tribes lived in Alaska before the arrival of Europeans, including the Aleut, Athabaskan, Eyak, Haida, Iñupiat, Tlingit, Tsimshian, and Yupik.

U.S. Secretary of State William H. Seward was enthusiastic about the idea of increasing the size of the United States. However, the 1867 purchase of Alaska, which he negotiated with Russia, was generally criticized until gold was discovered in the territory during the 1890s.

States. First of all, it was far away from the mainland United States. In addition, Alaska seemed to offer no resources to exploit for financial returns. This would change drastically over the next century.

The first official census was conducted in 1880 and reported a total of 33,426 people living in Alaska. Of these, all but 430 people were Native Americans.

Alaska was overseen by the U.S. army until 1876 and then by the U.S. Navy, which took charge of the territory in 1879. After gold was discovered in the Juneau region in 1880, a governor was appointed to Alaska under the Organic Act of 1884. The local administration, however, had little real power.

Missionaries who had come to Alaska in the 1870s exerted considerable influence. One was Sheldon Jackson, who introduced reindeer to Alaska. Jackson's goal was to help the Eskimos, whose primary source of food was seals. However, the seal population had been greatly reduced through the wanton hunting of seals, primarily by the British.

The first great influx of people from the mainland United States occurred during the Gold Rush of 1896. The gold was first discovered in the Klondike region of the Yukon in northwestern Canada. Although the Klondike gold rush ended in 1899 due to lack of new discoveries, gold was discovered in Nome, Alaska. Many of the prospectors who had gone to Canada decided to remain in Alaska on their way back. To regulate the activities in mining camps, Alaska developed its first criminal code in 1899.

In 1900, Alaska was awarded a territorial representative in the U.S. Congress. That same year, the city of Juneau replaced Sitka as Alaska's capital. In 1912, Alaska officially became a U.S. territory and a government was established. The U.S. government then began building the Alaska railroad from Seward to Fairbanks in 1915.

By then, gold mining had died out, but the fishing industry had advanced significantly, primarily to help feed all the miners. As a result, fishing became the state's major industry.

Nearly 65,000 people lived in Alaska by 1910. Alaska's population would decline somewhat over the years until World War II, which saw the U.S. military significantly increase its presence in Alaska to ward off a potential Japanese attack on the United States via Alaska's coastline. The Japanese did capture some of the Aleutian Islands in early 1942, but these were soon recaptured by the U.S. military.

Overall, during World War II, the military population in Alaska grew to more than 100,000. Meanwhile, the civilian population also grew as a robust economy near military posts attracted contractors and provided jobs.

Four gold prospectors pause on their way to the Yukon Territory, 1897. More than 100,000 prospectors passed through Alaska between 1896 and 1899, hoping to strike it rich.

The crew of a fishing boat shows off cod and halibut they caught off the coast of Alaska, 1920s. Today, commercial fishing remains an important part of the state's economy.

From 1913 to 1958, Alaska was governed by a territorial legislature, which passed many laws affecting Alaskans. Nevertheless, the U.S. government held most of the power over Alaskans.

Alaskans eventually began a movement to seek statehood. In anticipation of becoming a state, the territorial legislature passed an act authorizing a constitutional convention. Alaskans voted for 55 delegates from throughout the territory to meet in Fairbanks in 1955 to write a state constitution, which would take effect if Alaska became a state.

In 1958, the U.S. House of Representatives approved statehood for Alaska by a vote of 208 to 166. The U.S. Senate followed with its approval by a 64 to 20 vote. On July 7, 1958, President Dwight D. Eisenhower signed the Alaska Statehood Bill into law. In January 1959, Eisenhower announced that Alaska had become the 49th state of the United States. At last, Alaskans had full representation in the federal government.

The strongest earthquake ever recorded in North America, and the second strongest in the world, took place in Alaska on March 27, 1964. Measured at 9.2 on the Richter scale, the earthquake occurred in the Prince William Sound region of Alaska. In addition to causing the deaths of 114 people, the earthquake caused extensive damage in many of Alaskan cities. Overall the cost of the damage was estimated to be around $300 to $400 million in 1964 dollars.

In 1971 the U.S. Congress approved the Alaska Native Claims Settlement Act, which was created to resolve issues concerning native land claims in the state. Signed into law by President Richard M. Nixon on December 18, 1971, the act granted title to 40 million acres of land to Alaska natives, which amounted to approximately 10 percent of the state's territory. In addition, the act provided $962.5 million in payments to Native Americans, which was meant to stimulate economic development throughout the state. At the time, it was the largest lands claims settlement in U.S. history.

Although explorers had been searching for oil in Alaska since the 1890s, the largest oil field in North America was discovered at Prudhoe Bay in 1968. That oil field ranks among the twenty largest oil and gas fields in the world. The discovery of the field led to construction of the Trans-Alaska Pipeline from 1974 to 1977. The pipeline transports oil to the city of Valdez, where it is loaded onto ships that can transport the oil to refineries in other states.

In 1989 the oil tanker *Exxon Valdez* ran aground in Alaska's Prince William Sound. The shipwreck resulted in 11 million gallons of crude oil spilling into the water. It was the worst oil spill in American history at the time. The result was an environmental catastrophe as the spill moved on into the Gulf of Alaska. Overall, the spill impacted more than 1,300 miles of extremely remote and wild shoreline.

In 1994, a jury found the ship's captain and his employer, the Exxon Corporation (now ExxonMobil), guilty of **negligence**. The original amount of damages to be paid by Exxon was $507.5 billion, which was to go to 33,000 commercial fisherman and various other *plaintiffs*. The U.S. Supreme Court reduced the award to $2.5 billion in 2008, however.

An extensive cleanup effort was launched, which took many years to complete. In 2014 the U.S. government announced that 13 of the 32 wildlife populations, habitats, and other resources that had been damaged as a result of the spill were "fully recovered" or "very likely recovered." However, some species are listed as "not recovering," including a pod of orca whales and the Pacific herring, which was once a key part of a the state's commercial fishing operations. In the case of the orca pod, scientists have found that only one older female remains, and scientists believes this unique group of orcas will probably become extinct.

Government

Alaska's government operates under its constitution, which was ratified in 1956 and became effective with Alaska's statehood. The executive branch is headed by a governor and the secretary of state, who are elected for four-year terms. The governor appoints the heads of all of the various state departments, as well as many other officials. Alaska's governor is considered one of the most powerful governors in the United States.

Alaska has a bicameral legislature, consisting of the Senate and the House of Representatives. The Alaska House of Representatives includes forty representatives, who serve two-year terms; twenty senators serve in the Alaska Senate for four-year terms.

Like every other state, Alaska elects two members to the United States Senate. However, because of its relatively small population compared to most other states, Alaska has only one member in the U.S. House of Representatives. In the national election for the U.S. presidency, Alaska casts three electoral votes.

For many years the Democratic Party dominated Alaska's state politics but since 1966 the Republican Party has become dominant.

In addition to the typical state government that Alaska shares with many other states, another form of government that exists in Alaska is the tribal government. These governments exist in various forms throughout the state's vast rural areas.

Overall, the U.S. government recognizes 229 tribes in Alaska. A U.S. Supreme Court ruling known as the Venetie case sharply limited tribal governments' power in Alaska. Still, tribal governments do play a role in making decisions in many villages. For example, a 1999 Alaska Supreme Court ruling upheld the authority of tribes in handling child custody cases involving tribe members.

The Economy

Alaska's economy is dependent on four major factors: its location, climate, topography, and resources. Alaska has abundant natural resources, including oil, various minerals, forests, and fish. Oil and seafood are two of the major industries in Alaska. They primarily sell

A tanker is loaded with oil at the refinery in Valdez.

Sarah Louise Palin served as the ninth governor of Alaska from 2006 until her resignation in 2009. She was the Republican Party nominee for vice president in the 2008 presidential election, running with Arizona Senator John McCain. Palin has gone on to become a conservative political commentator and author.

their products to markets outside of Alaska.

Prior to Alaska becoming a state in 1959, the fishing and mining industries, along with the federal government, accounted for most of the state's jobs. However, since the 1960s when large oil reserves were discovered in Alaska, oil production has dominated the state's economy.

The oil companies actually only employ a few thousand people directly, but many more than that work in oil-related positions, such as oilfield services, construction activities, and pipeline operations. The state collects significant revenues from oil royalties and taxes paid to the state by oil companies.

Alaska's oil production, however, is falling and is expected to continue to decline over the years. In addition, much of the revenue from oil depends on worldwide oil prices, which can rise and fall depending on the available supply.

Despite the rise of Alaska's oil industry, the state's seafood industry remains a vital component of Alaska's economy. The industry employs about

9,000 people in the fishing industry and another 7,000 in the fish processing industry. The value of commercially caught fish in Alaska is estimated to be worth $1.7 billion a year. In addition, the fishing industry generates more than $100 million in state and local taxes annually.

Alaska is also home to large mining operations, including mining of zinc, gold, silver, and coal. On average Alaska' mineral production has a total annual value of more than $1 billion.

Another major supporter of Alaska's economy is the U.S. government. It has been estimated that approximately one-third of Alaskan jobs depend either directly or indirectly on federal spending. Each year, the federal government spends more than $12 billion in Alaska. Federal spending focuses on military and federal civilian agencies and on industries such as construction and health care. Part of the reason for the high level of federal spending in Alaska is because the U.S. government owns and manages a large part of Alaska's lands. Alaska also has several military bases.

The Trans-Alaska Pipeline, built in the 1970s, transports crude oil 800 miles (1,287 km) from Prudhoe Bay's oil fields to a seaport at Valdez.

After oil and natural gas, Alaska's most important export product is seafood. King crabs, salmon, and cod are among the main types of fish caught in the state's waters.

Some Famous Alaskans

Sydney Mortimer Laurence (1865–1940) was a landscape painter who is one of Alaska's most renowned artists. Although he was born in New York City, Laurence settled in Alaska around 1903, and painted many scenes of Alaska.

Jack London

Jack London (1876–1916) was an American author and journalist who gained worldwide celebrity for his short stories and novels. His most famous works, the adventure novels *Call of the Wild* and *White Fang*, are both based on his experiences in the Klondike during the Alaskan gold rush of 1897.

The first Native American movie star, Ray Mala (1906–1952), remains the most prolific film actor from Alaska. Born in the village of Candle, Mala starred in more than a dozen films, including the Academy Award-winning film *Eskimo* (1933), and also worked as a cinematographer.

John Ben "Benny" Benson Jr. (1913–1972), an Aleut born in Chignik, was thirteen years old when he won a 1927 contest to design the flag for the Alaska Territory. In 2013, the airport in Kodiak was named for Benny Benson.

Alaska-born Nora Marks Dauenhauer (b. 1927) is a scholar of the Tlingit language and traditions. She is also a poet and short-story writer. Her 2008 book *Russians in Tlingit America* won the American Book Award.

Tommy Moe (b. 1970) is a former ski racer who won the gold medal in downhill skiing and the silver medal in the super G event during the 1994 Winter Olympics in Lillehammer, Norway. Moe moved to Alaska during his teenage years to attend the Glacier Creek Ski Academy.

Jewel Kilcher (b. 1974) is an American singer-songwriter, producer, actress, and poet. Her grandfather, Yule Kilcher, was a delegate to the Alaska Constitutional Convention and a state senator, and she grew up on an 800-acre homestead in Homer. Jewel has won four Grammy Awards and sold more than 27 million records.

Jewel

Alaska's forestry or timber industry was the second-largest industry in Alaska during the 1970s. Since that time, the industry has declined signif icantly partly due to federal policies, shifting of land usage, and opposition from environmental groups looking to protect Alaska's forests.

Alaska is also internationally famous for its rugged beauty. As a result, tourism is a major industry. In 2014, nearly 2 million people visited Alaska, spending $3.9 billion. Overall the tourism industry provides approximately 46,000 jobs for Alaskans.

Alaska's employment growth since the 1970s has largely been in service industries. About half of all Alaskans are employed in trade and service jobs, such as working in retail stores and hospitals.

The People

Although whites make up the majority of the Alaskan population, the state includes a wide variety of ethnic groups, including many native Alaskans, such as the *Inuit*, the Aleut, and Tlingit. The primary connection between the many groups that live in Alaska is a sense of independence, toughness, and self-reliance, all of which are important qualities in a state that can face extremely harsh winters and where some people live in very remote areas.

Overall, not that many people live in Alaska. Despite its size, Alaska ranks 47 of the 50 states in population, ahead of only Wyoming, Vermont, and North Dakota. According to the U.S. Census Bureau, Alaska has a population of about 750,000 people. However, the state is growing, as the Census Bureau reported a 3.5 percent increase in the population from 2010 to 2015.

More men live in Alaska than women: according to the Census Bureau, approximately 53 percent of the population is male and 47 percent is female. Whites make up 67.3 percent of the population, compared to the nationwide average of 77.7 percent. In contrast, Alaska is home to a much higher percentage of American Indians and Alaskan natives at 14.7 percent of the population compared to the nationwide average of 1.2 percent.

African Americans make up only 3.9 percent of the population compared to 13.2 percent overall in the United States. In terms of the Asian population, Alaska has a slightly larger percentage of Asians at 5.4 percent compared to 4.8 percent in the nation as a whole. Hispanics make up approximately 6.6 percent of the population compared to 17.1 percent in the entire nation.

Major Cities

Although Alaska may be best known for its wilderness setting, the state

Mountains loom over Anchorage, the largest city in Alaska.

boasts three major cities. Located in south central Alaska, ***Anchorage*** is Alaska's largest city with a population of about 290,000 people. Roughly 40 percent of all Alaskans live in or near Anchorage.

Founded in 1914 as a railroad construction port for the Alaska Railroad, Anchorage is also one of the youngest cities in the United States. It is a major port, as more than 95 percent of all freight entering Alaska passes through Anchorage. Its primary industries are the military, government, petroleum, and tourism.

The next two largest cities in Alaska are ***Juneau*** and ***Fairbanks***. These two cities have populations so close in number, typically around 32,000 people, that they sometimes switch positions as Alaska's second-largest city. The difference in population between the two is typically only a few hundred people.

Juneau, nestled at the foot of Mount Juneau, is the state capital. It is located at the edge of the Gastineau Channel in the northern portion of the Inside Passage, a coastal route for

Often, small "float planes" that can land on and take off from lakes or other bodies of water are the most efficient way to travel between small communities in the interior of Alaska.

ships. Because there are no roads into Juneau, people travel there either by boat or airplane.

Juneau is sometimes referred to as Little San Francisco and is home to approximately one-half of the world's population of bald eagles. Juneau is a popular tourist destination in the summer. The majority of Juneau's population works in government, fishing, mining, and tourism.

Fairbanks is the largest city in the interior of Alaska and is located in the central Tanana Valley. Fairbanks is also the largest northern city of more than 20,000 people. It is a major center of commerce and trade for communities in the interior region of Alaska. Fairbanks is home to the University of Alaska-Fairbanks, the oldest of Alaska's universities, which attracts students from all over the world.

Since the beginning of World War II, Fairbanks has been a "military town," where 30 percent of all jobs in the city are generated by the military or related industries. Fairbanks is also a tourist destination, with most tourists arriving in the city via the railroad. Fairbanks is sometimes referred to as the Golden Heart City, a name attributed to its Gold Rush past.

Further Reading

Bernard, C.B. *Chasing Alaska: A Portrait of the Last Frontier Then and Now*. Guilford, Conn.: Lyons Press, 2013.

Muir, John. *Travels in Alaska*. LaVergne, Tenn.: Kessinger, 2012.

Thomas, William. *Alaska*. Milwaukee, Wis.: Gareth Stevens Pub., 2007.

Internet Resources

http://www.akhistorycourse.org

Alaska History and Cultural Studies provides students, teachers, and others interested in the state information about Alaska and its history.

http://alaska.gov

The official Web site of the state of Alaska that provides a wealth of information, from information on the state's government and economy to tourism and a Web page targeting young readers.

http://www.litsite.org/index.cfm

LitSite Alaska focuses on Alaskan life, culture, and history and features a special page for young people titled Alaska Kids.

 # Text-Dependent Questions

1. Which Alaskan river is best known for its enormous salmon run upstream to spawn?
2. Why was the U.S. purchase of Alaska considered a "folly"?
3. How many major migrations occurred in Alaska prior to the arrival of the Europeans and where did the people come from in each migration?

 # Research Project

The oil tanker *Exxon Valdez* ran aground in Alaska in 1989, resulting in the state's worst environmental disaster. Using your school library and the Internet, explore the impact that the accident had on the environment, citing its impact on various animal species, the land, and the water. Also explain how it impacted the local fishery industry. You can also detail the initial response and whether or not the accident resulted in changes to regulations concerning oil spill prevention, response, and cleanup efforts.

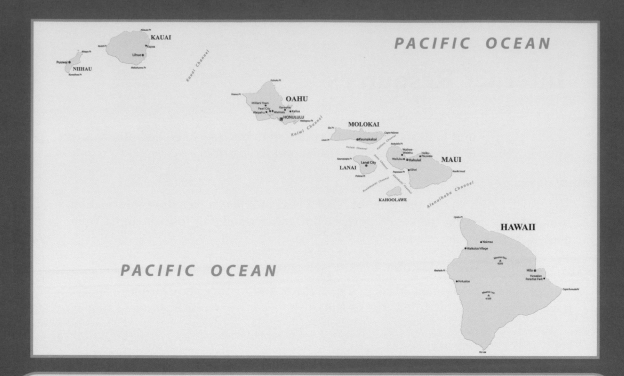

Hawaii at a Glance

Area: 10,931 sq mi (28,311 sq km).[1]
  (43rd largest state).
  Land: 6,423 sq mi (16,635 sq km)
  Water: 4,508 sq mi (11,676 sq km)
Highest elevation: Mauna Kea,
  13,796 feet (4,205 m)
Lowest elevation: shoreline, sea level

Statehood: Aug. 21, 1959 (50th state)
Capital: Honolulu

Population: 1,419,561
  (40th largest state)[2]

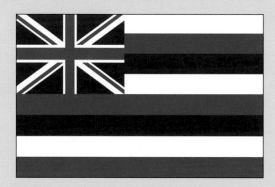

State nickname: the Aloha State
State bird: Nene (Hawaiian goose)
State flower: hibiscus (yellow)

[1] *U.S. Census Bureau*
[2] *U.S. Census Bureau, 2014 estimate*

Hawaii

The state of Hawaii has long been a dream destination for vacationers from the U.S. mainland. With numerous beautiful beaches, lush flora and fauna, and almost perfect temperatures, Hawaii is a tropical paradise. It is also a place with a unique history. Unlike the states of the mainland, Hawaii has strong Asian and Polynesian cultural influences that remain to this day.

Geography

Located in the Central Pacific Ocean about 2,468 miles (3,972 km) from the coast of California, Hawaii is the only state made up entirely of islands. The Hawaiian *archipelago* is the most remote and longest archipelago in the world. It spans 1,523 miles (2,451 km) from the Island of Hawaii in the southeast to the Kure *Atoll*, or Ocean Island, in the northwest.

Overall, the state of Hawaii recognizes 137 islands in the Hawaiian archipelago as being part of the state. Only seven of the islands are inhabited year-round, however.

Hawaii's eight main islands are Hawaii (called the "Big Island"), Oahu, Maui, Kauai, Molokai, Lanai, Niihau, and Kahoolawe. The main islands are located at the southeastern end of the long island chain. The rest of the islands are primarily rocky *islets*, reefs, shoals, and atolls. They are called the Northwestern Hawaiian Islands.

All of the Hawaiian Islands were formed by volcanic activity. They are actually the tips of gigantic submerged mountains, known as *seamounts*.

The islands in the chain, known as the Hawaiian-Emperor seamount chain, are progressively older from the southeast to the northwest. The youngest seamount in the chain, Loihi, is an active volcano that has reached a height of 3,280 feet (1,000 m) above the ocean's surface. The oldest major island in the chain is Kauai, which is believed to be approximately six million years old.

The topography of the Hawaiian islands varies somewhat from island to island. However, the islands share the

Words to Understand in This Chapter

archipelago—a group of islands.
atoll—a reef, island, or chain of island formed of coral and in a ring shape.
dormant—temporarily inactive.
indigenous—something that is native to a particular place.
islet—a small island.
martial law—establishment of a military government, often involving the suspension of ordinary laws and democratic procedures.
referendum—a general vote by people on a political question .
seamount—an underwater mountain formed by volcanic activity.

Waimanalo Bay is lined by the longest uninterrupted white-sand beach on Oahu.

Pali Notches on Oahu is a popular spot for hikers.

Surfers come from all over the world to ride the waves at Pe'ahi, on the north coast of Maui. Waves here can reach as high as 50 feet (15 m).

Red hot lava from Hawaii's Kilauea volcano flows into the Pacific Ocean.

common traits of containing both beautiful beaches at sea level and mountainous terrain. Overall, the entire state has 750 miles (1,200 km) of coastline and a total land area of approximately 6,423 square miles (16,635 sq km).

The Big Island of Hawaii has an area of 4,028 square miles (10,433 sq km) and is the youngest of Hawaii's main islands. The island boasts the highest mountains in the state. Mauna Kea rises 13,796 feet (4,205 m) above sea level and is the tallest mountain in the world if measured from its base in the depths of the ocean. Although it is located in a tropical climate, Mauna Kea is sometimes called the "white mountain" because of its snowcapped peak. Another mountain, Mauna Loa, is 13,678 feet (4,169 m) above sea level.

The Big Island of Hawaii is still continuing to grow due to its active and erupting volcanoes, most of which are located in the Hawaii Volcanoes National Park. Active volcanoes on the big island include Mauna Loa, or "Long Mountain" in Hawaiian, and its

 Did You Know?

Because of Hawaii's isolated location and tropical climate, its diverse plant and animal population includes many species found only on the islands. Unfortunately, many of these species are endangered, and Hawaii has the most endangered species of any state in the country.

neighbor, the Kilauea volcano, which is the most active volcano on all of the islands and one of the most active in the world. Lava oozing from Kilauea has created 600 acres of new land since 1983.

Maui is the next island north of the Big Island and is the second largest island in the state at 727 square miles (1,883 sq km). Maui has lush rainforests and fertile soil due to past volcanic eruptions. The island also has mountains. The Haleakala volcano found in the southeastern region of the island has a crater that measures 3,000 feet (914 m) deep and 21 miles (34 km) in circumference.

Panoramic mountains tower over Kahului, the largest community on Maui.

A distinctive geological feature found on Maui is the Dragon's Teeth coastline. Found along the desolate coastline of south Maui, the Dragon's Teeth was formed by lava from the West Maui volcano. As the lava flowed into the sea, strong wind and waves pushed the lava back, forming sharp and curved spires as the lava cooled on the shoreline.

Heading north, the next island is Oahu, which is 597 square miles (1,546 sq km) in size. The island's distinctive geological feature is that it lies between two mountain ranges formed by two shield volcanoes: Waianae in the west and Koolau in the east.

Shield volcanoes are typically formed completely by very fluid lava flows. They are named shield volcanoes because of their large size and low profile, which makes them look similar to a shield lying on the ground. More than 100 ridges extend from the spines of these two ranges on Oahu, forming both lush valleys and high mountain vistas.

Overall, Oahu is famous for the numerous volcanic cones found all over the island, all of which are ***dormant***. Oahu also features the Punchbowl Crater, called Puowaina, typically translated as "Hill of Sacrifice," by the native Hawaiians. Formed about 100,000 years ago, the crater was once used by the native people as an altar for human sacrifices.

Oahu also features the Diamond Head Crater, an extinct volcano at the edge of the south shore, and the Halona Blowhole, which is a natural geyser that shoots seawater more than

Scenic view of Diamond Head and Waikiki Beach on Oahu.

A waterfall drops into colorful Waimea Canyon, also known as the Grand Canyon of the Pacific. This spectacular canyon is about ten miles (16 km) long and up to 3,000 feet (900 m) deep.

The rocky region known as the Garden of the Gods, or Keahiakawelo, is located on the island of Lanai.

30 feet in the air. Hawaii in general does not have many rivers. The largest, the Kaukonahua Stream, is on Oahu and flows for 33 miles (53 km).

Kauai, 552 square miles (1,430 sq km) in size, is the most fertile of the Hawaiian Islands. The island's center features lush, mountainous regions.

Significant geological features of Kauai include Waimea Canyon, which is known as the Grand Canyon of the Pacific. Located on the western side of the island, the canyon is around ten miles (16 km) long with the deepest canyons 3,000 feet deep (900 m). Mount Waialeale, a shield volcano in the center of Kauai, rises 5,066 feet (1,544 m) above sea level. The island also has gorges as deep as 5,148 feet (1,569 m). Kauai's Na Pali Coast has 17 miles (27 km) of coastline featuring cliffs that rise thousands of feet in the air.

Lanai is the sixth-largest island in the Hawaiian chain, with a land area of 140 square miles (363 sq km). More arid and dryer than other islands in the chain, the island's highest point is Lanaihale, which stands at 3,370 feet (1,027 m). The island, formerly called Pineapple Island, also features the Palawai Basin, which is a fertile plain where pineapples once grew.

Lanai also features the Garden of the Gods, also called Keahiakawelo. Located on the northwest side of the island, the strange rock garden features unusual rock formations and red dirt that sometimes compared to the landscape on the planet Mars.

Molokai is approximately 261 squares miles (676 sq km) in size, making it the fifth-largest island in Hawaii. Located 25 miles (40 km) southeast of Oahu and eight miles (13 km) from Maui, Molokai is at the center of the Hawaiian Island chain. Molokai was formed by the Mauna Loa volcano on its west end and the Kamakou volcano in the east.

Molokai features pristine beaches and towering sea cliffs along its 88-mile (142-km) coastline. The cliffs on the North Shore Pali are the tallest in the world, standing at 3,600 to 3,900 feet (1,097 to 1,189 m). The highest point on the island is Mt. Kamakou, which stands at 4,970 feet (1,515 m)

Did You Know?

Hawaii is a popular place to make movies. The huge spires and cliffs of Na Pali Coastline on the northwest side of Kauai served as the backdrop for the movie *Jurassic Park*. The island of Molokai and its sea cliffs, which are among the highest in the world, were the backdrop for *Jurassic Park 3*.

above sea level. The island also features the Kalaupapa Peninsula jutting out from the north central part of the island.

Kahoolawe, at 45 square miles (117 sq km), is the smallest of the major islands. Located about seven miles (11 km) southwest of the island of Maui, Khaoolawe is a relatively dry island for the tropics with about 26 inches (66 cm) of rainfall each year. The island's highest point is the Lua Makika crater at the summit of Pu'u Moaulanui, which stands 1,477 feet (450 m) above sea level.

Approximately one-fourth of Kahoolawe is eroded down to sapro-litic hardpan soil, a soft and highly decomposed porous rock formed by chemical weathering. Access to the island is only available to native Hawaiians for cultural and spiritual purposes, or to those who receive permits to visit for scientific or educational reasons.

Niihau is approximately 68 square miles (176 sq km) in size and lies about 18 miles (29 km) west of Kauai. Niihau is the youngest of the major Hawaiian Islands at about 4.9 million years old. The smallest of Hawaii's inhabited islands, Niihau features a dormant volcano and its highest point is Paniau, which stands at 1,280 feet (390 m).

Niihau also features playa lakes, which are hollow depressions in the ground that contain water at only certain times of the year. Theses lakes are noted wetland habitats for several bird species.

Although the weather in Hawaii varies somewhat between the islands, they typically have a mild and relatively stable climate that features high summer temperatures around 88°F

(31°C) and lows during the winter in the lower 80s. The islands feature both wet and dry seasons, with the island of Kauai having the second-highest average rainfall on Earth, at 460 inches (1,168 cm) per year.

History

Some historians believe that Hawaii was probably a stopping point for various peoples traveling the oceans before Polynesians from the South Pacific finally landed on the islands. Although the exact dates of their arrival are unknown, researchers estimate that they probably arrived between 300 and 500 CE in large voyaging canoes.

The first Polynesians to arrive in Hawaii were believed to have come from the Marquesas Islands. The first main settlement likely occurred around 500 CE on the Big Island of Hawaii, where archaeologist found an early *heiau*, or temple.

By 900 CE, all of the major Hawaiian Islands were occupied by people. A second Ploynesian migration occurred around 1100 from the

Thousands of petroglyphs were carved into lava rocks by the original inhabitants of the big island of Hawaii around 1,700 years ago.

Society Islands.

Around 1400, the Polynesian occupants of the islands were conquered and enslaved by Tahitian explorers. A Tahitian priest named Pa'ao started a lineage of high priests, called the

In 1778, Captain James Cook commanded the first European ship that landed on the Hawaiian islands. The famed explorer of the Pacific was killed during a return visit to Hawaii in 1779.

"kahuna nui," who served as ruling kings on each of the islands. The individual island governments typically had a king assisted by a chief minister and a high priest.

The majority of the people in Hawaii at this time were commoners known as *makaainana*. They did the hard work, paid taxes, and served as warriors. Another group known as the *kauwa*, or outcasts, were most likely slaves.

Europeans visited Hawaii in January 1778 when British Captain James Cook (1728–1779) and his expedition arrived on the islands of Kauai and Niihau. Each of the islands at that time still retained their own kings. Cook returned in 1779 to the Big Island, but was killed when he chased after a stolen rowboat.

It was not until 1810 that a man named Kamehameha I (1758–1819) conquered all of the islands and placed them under one rule, establishing the Kingdom of Hawaii. Just ten years after Hawaii became a united country, missionaries from New England and elsewhere arrived. At the time the Hawaiian language had no written form. The missionaries helped native Hawaiians develop a written language during the 1820s.

European contact, however, had a devastating impact on Hawaii's population. In 1779, the population was estimated to be between 250,000 and

1 million people. By 1848, there were approximately only 88,000 native Hawaiian Islanders due to the introduction of contagious diseases, such as measles and cholera, for which the natives had no immunity.

Hawaii's first constitution was created by Kamehameha III in 1842. That same year, U.S. President John Tyler officially recognized the Kingdom of Hawaii. The growing interest in Hawaii by the United States and Europeans eventually led Kamehameha III to allow foreigners to begin purchasing land and establishing businesses on the islands.

By the 1840s, the towns of Lahaina and Honolulu were the busiest whaling ports in the Pacific. Foreign laborers also began to arrive in Hawaii to work in the sugar and pineapple fields. Meanwhile, valuable sandalwood trees were stripped from the mountain forests on Hawaii, Oahu, Molokai, and Kauai.

By the 1890s, foreigners had gained control of approximately 90 percent of Hawaiian lands. In 1891, King Kalakaua, who was an elected

This statue of Lili'uokalani, the last Hawaiian monarch, stands outside the state capitol building in Honolulu.

king, died. His sister Lili'uokalani became queen of the islands.

On January 17, 1893, the Hawaiian monarchy was overthrown

Sanford B. Dole was born in Honolulu to Christian missionaries. He was an advisor to the Hawaiian monarchs, and later served as the first president of the Hawaiian Republic from 1894 to 1898. After the U.S. annexation of Hawaii, Dole was appointed the first governor of the territory.

by a group headed by Lorrin Thurston, who had become the Hawaiian minister of the interior, and a group of American businessmen. Although the U.S. government did not support the coup at first, the United States eventually supported the establishment of a government formed by Thurston, Sanford B. Dole, and others with ties to the United States. From 1894 to 1898, the country was known as the Republic of Hawaii.

On July 7, 1898, the United States officially took control over the Hawaiian islands after President William McKinley signed the Newlands Resolution, which declared the annexation of the islands. On February 22, 1900, the Hawaiian islands were organized as a U.S. territory. Sanford Dole, formerly president of the Republic, was appointed the first governor of the territory.

Over the years, sugar plantations greatly expanded and some of the sugar companies diversified into transportation, banking, and real estate. Overall, most of the power in Hawaii was in the hands of the "Big Five" corporations: Castle & Cooke, Alexander & Baldwin, C. Brewer & Co., American Factors (which became Amfac), and Theo H. Davies & Co. These companies had so much power that Hawaii was basically an oligarchy—a state where a small group of wealthy people control everything.

Hawaii played a central role in the U.S. decision to enter World War II when Japan attacked the U.S. naval base at Pearl Harbor on the island of Oahu on December 7, 1941. Pearl Harbor had been a strategic military base since the Spanish-American War of 1898. Following the attack, Hawaii was placed under *martial law* until the

(Right) The American battleship USS Arizona burns furiously after her forward ammunition magazine exploded during the Japanese attack on Pearl Harbor, December 7, 1941. The surprise attack on Pearl Harbor succeeded in eliminating the U.S. Navy's battleship force as a threat to Japanese expansion in the Pacific. The United States immediately declared war on Japan, becoming fully engaged in the Second World War. (Bottom) The USS Arizona Memorial, built in 1962 over the sunken remains of the battleship, commemorates the more than 2,500 Americans who were killed during the Pearl Harbor raid, including over 1,100 sailors on the Arizona.

end of the war in 1945. The military facilities at Pearl Harbor also served as America's base of operations in the Pacific theatre of the war.

On March 18, 1959, U.S. President Dwight D. Eisenhower signed the Hawaii Admission Act, which provided for Hawaii to become a state. In a *referendum,* 93 percent of the people living in Hawaii voting for statehood. Hawaii became the 50th state on August 21, 1959.

Although Hawaii benefitted from statehood, the U.S. seizure of the islands had long been a controversial issue among native Hawaiians. Many saw the takeover as illegal, and despaired as Hawaiian customs and traditions were lost in the years following Hawaii's annexation to the United States. Many Hawaiians also complained that they had suffered various forms of repression over the years. By the 1960s, a Hawaiian Renaissance

The Hawaii State Capitol building in Honolulu, which houses the state legislature, opened in 1969.

Ali'iolani Hale, or House of the Heavenly King, was built in 1874 as a royal palace. Today it houses Hawaii's Supreme Court. A gold-leaf statue of Kamehameha stands at the entrance.

movement had developed. It was intended to restore Hawaiian language, culture, and identity.

Government

The Kingdom of Hawaii was a constitutional monarchy, established in 1840. A constitutional monarchy is one in which the king or queen is the head of state, but the ability to create and pass laws and legislation rests with an elected body of representatives. Today, however, Hawaii's government is similar to other U.S. states. The government is divided into three branches: the executive, legislative, and judiciary.

The state's executive powers are

Daniel Inouye (1924–2012) represented Hawaii in the U.S. Senate from 1963 to 2012. A hero of World War II who earned the Medal of Honor, Inouye was the first Japanese American to serve in Congress.

held in the governor's office, which includes both the governor and lieutenant governor. These are the only statewide elected officials in all of Hawaii. The governor and lieutenant governor are elected for four-year terms and can only serve two terms. The lieutenant governor also serves in the capacity of secretary of state.

The governor appoints officials for about twenty departments. Department heads serve as long as the elected governor is in office unless otherwise dismissed by the governor. The governor also appoints justices to the Hawaiian Supreme Court and the appellate courts, which hear appeals to cases presented in other lower courts. Court appointees must be approved by the Hawaiian senate.

Hawaii's legislative branch has 25 senators and 51 representatives across the various districts covering the inhabited islands. State senators and legislators are elected by district voters. State representatives serve two-year terms, and state senators serve four-year terms. They are not limited to how many terms they can serve. The legislative branch's duties include creating legislation and laws for the state.

Local governments within the state are divided into four counties, which can also act as municipalities. These counties are the City and County of Honolulu, Maui County, Hawaii County, and Kauai County. These governments typically include a mayor and a council.

Hawaii is represented in the federal government by two senators and four members of the U.S. House of Representatives. Hawaii is primarily considered a Democratic state because it votes for candidates from the Democratic Party in most presidential elections. The state voted for the Republican Party presidential candidates in 1971 and 1984.

Although Hawaii has been a U.S. state for nearly 60 years, Hawaiian sovereignty remains an issue in the state. In the early 1990s, Hawaii's two U.S. Senators, Daniel Inouye and Daniel Akaka, headed an effort that led to the "Apology Resolution." Signed by President Bill Clinton on November 12, 1993, the resolution offered an official U.S. apology to native Hawaiians for the overthrow of the Kingdom of Hawaii in 1893. A bill was also introduced to establish a legal framework for the formation of a Native Hawaiian government.

Former U.S. Senator Daniel Akaka is applauded during a ceremony at the state capitol building.

Students perform a traditional dance at the Polynesian Cultural Center in La'ie, on the northern shore of Oahu. The center is a theme park and living history museum operated on the Hawaii campus of Brigham Young University.

Tourists pose with flowing lava during a hike near Kilauea volcano. Hawaii Volcanoes National Park, located on the big island, attracts more than 2.5 million tourists each year.

A majority of the approximately 200,000 descendants of **indigenous** Hawaiians voted in 1996 to establish some form of self-government. Two years later in August 1998, protesters marked the 100th anniversary of the U.S. annexation of Hawaii by marching in Washington, D.C. to demand full independence from the United States.

Senator Akaka introduced a bill in 2000, known as the Akaka bill, that would provide for official recognition of native Hawaiians and give them the same legal rights as federally recognized Native American tribes. However, this bill was never passed in Congress.

Groups also have been formed with the intention of highlighting Hawaii as an occupied nation. The ultimate goal of these groups, which include the Hawaiian Kingdom Government, is to regain Hawaii's complete independence from the United States.

In June 2014, the U.S. Department of Interior announced that it was taking steps to consider

In December 2014, David Ige took office as Hawaii's governor. He was born in Pearl City, and previously served in the state senate.

reestablishing a government-to-government relationship between the federal government and the native Hawaiian community. The decision was made in response to ongoing requests from the community and from Hawaii's congressional delegation and state leaders. The relationship would not consider the possibility of Hawaii becoming an independent nation, however.

The Economy

The primary drivers of Hawaii's economy are tourism and the U.S. military. Tourism contributes about $14 billion to the state's economy each year. It also contributes more than $1 billion a

Some Famous Hawaiians

Lili'uokalani (1838–1917) became queen of the Hawaiian Islands in 1891 and formally abdicated the throne in 1895, two years after a provisional government headed by Americans took control, making her the last Hawaiian monarch.

Duke Kahanamoku (1890–1968) was an athlete who represented the United States in the 1912 and 1920 Olympic Games. He won a gold medal in freestyle and relay swimming events. An excellent surfer, he also helped to popularize the sport among mainland Americans.

Duke Kahanamoku

Hiram Leon Fong (1906–2004), the son of a Chinese immigrant to Hawaii, became the first Asian American to serve in the U.S. Senate when he was elected to represent Hawaii in 1959.

Born in Honolulu, novelist and writer Lois Lowry (b. 1937) has won two Newbery Medals, which are awarded each year to honor the most distinguished contribution to American literature for children.

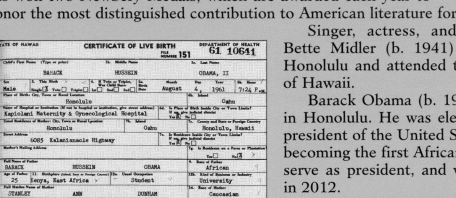

Barack Obama's official Hawaiian birth certificate.

Singer, actress, and comedienne Bette Midler (b. 1941) was born in Honolulu and attended the University of Hawaii.

Barack Obama (b. 1961) was born in Honolulu. He was elected the 44th president of the United States in 2008, becoming the first African American to serve as president, and was re-elected in 2012.

Pop singer Bruno Mars (b. 1985) has won two prestigious Grammy Awards and was named to *Time* magazine's list of the 100 most influential people in the world in 2011.

year in state tax revenue. Overall, tourism represents nearly one-quarter of the state's entire economy.

Ever since Pearl Harbor was established as a military base in 1874, the U.S. military has played a major role in Hawaii's economy. Approximately 10 percent of Hawaii's population is made up of military personnel and their families. The military also employs more civilians in Hawaii than any other industry. The military creates more than 102,000 jobs for residents and contributes more than $14 billion to the state's economy each year.

Hawaii also has a vibrant agricultural industry. For years sugar and

The U.S. Navy base at Pearl Harbor remains one of the most important American military facilities in the Pacific.

This sugar processing facility is operated by the Hawaiian Commercial and Sugar Company in Puunene, on the island of Maui. The Hawaiian Commercial and Sugar company was founded nearly 150 years ago; today, it is Hawaii's largest farm, with 36,000 acres under cultivation.

Taro fields in Hanalei Valley on Kauai. Taro is a root vegetable that is commonly used in native Hawaiian cuisine.

pineapple plantations were the backbone of Hawaii's agricultural industry. Due to cutbacks and closures based on factors such as rising production costs and market prices, these industries are not as strong in Hawaii as they once were. Many former sugar plantations are now used to grow Kona coffee, macadamia nuts, tropical fruits, and vegetables. These are now the primary crops for Hawaii's food processing industry.

Floriculture, or the cultivation of flowers, is also thriving due to the numerous tropical flowers and plants that grow in Hawaii. Many of Hawaii's flowers are exported throughout the United States. Eucalyptus trees are also grown to supply pulp for paper manufacturing in Japan, and bamboo is grown due to its popularity for use in such products as flooring, fencing, and furniture.

The construction industry is the fourth-largest private industry in Hawaii, after tourism, real estate, and health care. Construction adds some $4 billion to the Hawaiian economy and provides 32,000 jobs. Commercial fishing is also an important contributor to the economy.

The People

Hawaii has been a popular place to live since the start of the twentieth century. In 1900, the state's population stood at 154,000, but rose by nearly 25 percent to 191,874 by 1910.

Over the years many people have decided to move to Hawaii, primarily because of its great climate and natural beauty. The most limiting factor in Hawaii's population growth is the high cost of living.

According to the U.S. Census Bureau, Hawaii is the 40th largest state in terms of population, with more than 1.4 million residents.

Oahu has the most people with a population of about 976,000, followed by the Big Island of Hawaii, which has about 185,000 people. Kauai, with 67,000 people, is the only other island with a sizable population.

Hawaii is home to a wide range of ethnic groups. Whites make up almost a quarter of the population, which is far below the national average of 72.4

The skyline of Honolulu, the capital city of Hawaii, includes hotels and resorts on Waikiki Beach.

Aerial view of Hilo, the largest community on the Big Island of Hawaii. About 43,000 people live in Hilo.

percent. Hawaii also has a much smaller African American or black population than the U.S. as a whole, at 1.6 percent compared to an average of 12.6 percent throughout the nation.

On the other end of the spectrum, Hawaii has the highest percentage of Asian Americans, at nearly 39 percent. On average, Asian Americans make up only 4.6 percent of the entire U.S. population.

Obviously, the state also has the highest ratio of Native Hawaiian and other Pacific Islanders, with 10 percent of Hawaii's population falling into that Census Bureau category. The state's Hispanic/Latino population stands at 8.9 percent, approximately half the national average.

Major Cities

Honolulu is the largest city in Hawaii, home to 371,657 people in 2014. Located on the island of Oahu, Honolulu has more than seven times the population of the next largest city,

Pearl City, also located on Oahu.

Honolulu is the state's capital. Its name means "sheltered harbor" or "calm port." The city is a major hub for international business and the major financial center in the state.

With a population of 47,698, *Pearl City* lies just north of Honolulu. It is located on the north shore of Pearl Harbor. The Pearl Harbor National Wildlife Refuge is nearby.

The state's other larger cities are *Kailua*, also on the island of Oahu, and *Hilo*, on the Big Island of Hawaii. Both cities have populations under 50,000.

Kailua means "two seas" or "two currents" and draws its name either from two lagoons in the surrounding district or the two major currents that run through Kailua Bay. Hilo is home to Merrie Monarch Festival, a yearly, weeklong festival honoring the ancient and modern hula, a dance developed on the Hawaiian Islands by the Polynesians.

Further Reading

Haley, James L. *Captive Paradise: A History of Hawaii*. New York, NY: St. Martin's Press, 2014.

Maraniss, David. *Barack Obama: The Story*. New York, NY: Simon & Schuster, 2012.

Siler, Julia Flynn. *Lost Kingdom: Hawaii's Last Queen, the Sugar Kings and America's First Imperial Adventure*. New York, NY: Atlantic Monthly Press, 2012.

Internet Resources

https://www.hawaiianhistory.org

> The Hawaiian Historical Society's Web site includes information on the history of Hawaii, images of selected items from the society's photo collection, and a list of links for further research into the state of Hawaii.

https://portal.ehawaii.gov

> The official Web site of the Aloha State includes information on the government, business, state data, photographs, visitor information, and more.

http://www.gohawaii.com/en/#/

> Hawaii's official tourism site.

 # Text-Dependent Questions

1. How were the Hawaiian Islands formed? What is the most active volcano in Hawaii?
2. What role did Hawaii play in the United States entering World War II?

 # Research Project

Do some extra research and write a short paper on how Hawaii went from being an independent nation to a U.S. territory to a state.

Index

Numbers in **bold italics** refer to captions.

Series Glossary of Key Terms

bicameral—having two legislative chambers (for example, a senate and a house of representatives).

cede—to yield or give up land, usually through a treaty or other formal agreement.

census—an official population count.

constitution—a written document that embodies the rules of a government.

delegation—a group of persons chosen to represent others.

elevation—height above sea level.

legislature—a lawmaking body.

precipitation—rain and snow.

term limit—a legal restriction on how many consecutive terms an office holder may serve.